Telling Tales of Dusk

Telling Tales of Dusk

POEMS BY

TERRI KIRBY ERICKSON

Press 53
Winston-Salem, NC

Press 53
PO Box 30314
Winston-Salem, NC 27130

First Edition

Copyright © 2009 by Terri Kirby Erickson

Cover design by Kevin Watson

Cover art by Stephen White, Copyright © 2009 by Stephen White

Cover photograph of art by Dan Rossi

Printed on acid-free paper

ISBN 978-0-9824416-3-3

ACKNOWLEDGMENTS

Grateful acknowledgement is made to the editors of the following publications in which the poems noted first appeared: *Bay Leaves*, "Bobbing for Apples"; *Blue Fifth Review*, "Sleeping Alone"; *Broad River Review*, "Seventeen," "A Mother Laments Her Daughter's Tattoo," "Madeline Parmenter," "Salesman"; *Christian Science Monitor*, "Queen Anne's Lace"; *CowboyPoetry.com, 2009*, "Oak Tree," *Dead Mule School of Southern Literature, 2008*, "Smoke and Mirrors," "Alafair," "A Day in the Life," "Golden Years," "Oak Tree"; *Old Mountain Press*, "Brunson Elementary School" (*Looking Back*), "Squirrel" (*In the Yard*), "Queen's Court" (*Southern Mist*); *Parent:Wise Austin*, "Washing My Baby's Hair Over the Kitchen Sink"; *Pinesong*, "Madison's Picture"; Northwest Cultural Council International Juried Art & Poetry Exhibition 2006 and 2007, "My Father," "Devotion"; *Pisgah Review*, "County Fair"; *Relief: A Quarterly Christian Expression*, "Minnows"; *Silver Boomer Books*, "Druid Hill Drive"; *Smoking Poet*, "Delta Blues"; *Thread Count*, "The Belle of Bourbon Street"; *Voices and Vision*, "Butter Mints," "Daisy Chain"; *Wild Goose Poetry Review*, "Assisted Living," "A Rancher Buries His Wife."

for my mother and father,
with love

Contents

I

II

V

I

County Fair

Pulled like rotten teeth from the open mouths
of mineshafts, massive pyramids of gleaming
coal dot the landscape of Kanawha County.
Coal dust fine and black as pulverized midnight,
covers everything for miles. Rows of ramshackle
houses kneel by the river like washer women
with their knees in river muck, and jagged
mountains cut the slate-gray sky

to ribbons. But the Kanawha River is long
and winding, and leads to a lone Ferris wheel
rising up from the bottomland, jaunty
as an Easter bonnet. Its rainbow-colored gondolas
call to mind a different tune than the dismal dirges
of Black Lung and White Damp. They carry the sound
of children's laughter through the ground
and into the mines, like light.

Star Lite Motel

He knew it was just an ordinary motel on the side of a busy highway, nothing special about it, really. There were a billion more like it, lying along curbs like bums on a park bench. But when dusk settled on the roof like a soft, blue cloth, rubbing away the harsh edges and inelegant angles,

and the neon sign flashed the words, *Star Lite Motel,* it never failed to move him. There was something magical

in the name, as if the tired old building still pulsed with possibility, as if it were more than a place for afternoon trysts or weary travelers, worn out from hours on the road. As he sat behind the desk night after night, reading the newspaper or watching the miniature television set

hanging from the ceiling, he dispensed keys to characters of every age and description, while keeping an eye out

for certain people. He recognized them right off, as soon as they came through the door—the ones who stopped because the sign drew them in. They had an air of expectation and a lighter step, as if the world weighed less heavily

on their shoulders, like something wonderful waited just around the bend. Sometimes they were alone, but not always. It didn't matter. To them he gave the best rooms, the ones near the office and the ice machine, where the name *Star Lite Motel* shone through the windows like a benediction.

SMOKE AND MIRRORS

Once, dressed in black, a cigarette dangling
from your lips, you rolled down the window

of your car and called to me, voices blaring
from your radio like backup singers. The boy

I was talking to dissolved, tablet-like,
in the watered down scenery of the things

that were not you—the sky, the ground,
buildings along the road, the books I carried.

There was only your face behind those mirrored
sunglasses, a car door opening, the seat beside you.

BOBBING FOR APPLES

On road trips, she used to pop her boys
on the head with the sharp end of a high-heeled
shoe when they got too rowdy. You can't do
that sort of thing anymore, but it sure was
effective. Anyway, she never hit them
too hard, just a quick tap so they'd know
she meant business. Keeping four boys out
of their father's hair while he was driving
down the highway was a big responsibility
and she took it serious as a heart attack.
She loved her children but Lord forgive
her, she was crazy in love with that husband
of hers from the first time she saw him hoist
a ham on a butcher's block in the general
store he ran in West Virginia, the muscles
in his arms nearly ripping his shirt right
down the sleeves. It was embarrassing
for a church-going woman like herself
who wouldn't think of leaving the house
without a good girdle and the perfect
pill box hat, to nearly swoon with
palpitations when her own husband
walked in the room, but that was about
the size of it. She took pains to cover it
up as best she could, but everybody with
eyes in their heads knew it. Folks figured
it was her Mediterranean blood firing
all that passion, especially when she got
to swinging her shoe around the family
Buick, four dark heads bobbing like they
were searching the back seat for apples.

A Mother Laments
Her Daughter's Tattoo

She remembers the perfect flesh of her newborn child,
cell after cell of flawless skin, soft and pink as rose petals.

The ingratitude of it, she thinks, to mar that perfection
with mossy green ink, the color of mold creeping

up a wall, when soon enough the years will crease
and fold it, dry its dewy surface like wringing a wet

sponge. They are obscene, these man-made markings
the blatant vandalism of a pristine creation. It is graffiti

in a sanctuary, shoe prints on a wedding gown. To pay
for such defilement, to sit docile for redecoration,

is an act of self-destruction she cannot comprehend but must
accept—although forgive me, she says, if it takes a while.

Butter Mints

An old woman lived across
the street in a house so small
and square it might have been
a handkerchief, neatly folded,
in the pocket of its own front
porch. She was skinny as a switch,
hump-backed and liver-spotted,
the veins in her hands fat
as earthworms. She wore floral
patterned dresses with buttons
round and white as moons,
high-topped shoes triple-tied
with extra-long laces, and she
was no fool. On the kitchen
counter, she stacked her tins
of butter mints, homemade,
in baby blanket colors—pale
pinks, lemon yellows, sea-foam
greens. They drew us in like
beacons, eager to mop, dust
or sweep, in exchange for which
she doled them out, one at a time,
like solid gold doubloons.

QUEEN ANNE'S LACE

Queen Anne's lace dandies up
a ditch, like embroidered hankies
in a farmer's pocket.

Such tiny seed-pearl petals
seem hand-sewn by
seraphim to their purple

centers—yet they thrive
in common places, fine as tatted
borders, blanket-stitched to burlap.

ALAFAIR

She stood in the elevator of the Hotel Monteleone,
with its antique overhead lamp flickering
and its mercurial mechanizations, wherein it may
or may not stop at your particular floor. It was packed
with party-goers having spent hours of debauched

revelry on the streets of New Orleans, where booze
flowed in manna-like abundance and blues pounded

bodies like a butcher's hammer, tenderizing the toughened
shell of every base emotion. Raw and inside-out,
some reached for oblivion in whatever way

presented itself, sex or drink or darker sins, as long
as it stopped the pain. Their clothes reeked of cigarettes

and secretions, their mouths agape with falsetto laughter
that pierced her ears and drove her into a corner,
clutching her pink wrap, draped lightly as a child's

arm across her bare shoulders. Alafair wanted nothing
more than to step out of her mother's stiletto heels
and run through the twisted alleys and cobbled

streets of the French Quarter, all the way to Point au Fer—
but it was too late now for any such escape. The elevator

stopped; people made way for her to pass, which she did,
sweeping by them like a queen. Head held high, spine
straight as a steel bar, she crossed the threshold of an ancient
lift, long accustomed to delivering young women
to rich men's doors like freshly powdered beignets.

MINNOWS

A school of minnows
makes its way upstream, like mercury
moving under glass. Swimming in tight formation, they turn
together in a single fluid motion, their fins sheer as stockings draped
across their backs. So alike in every way, they might be mirrored
images of one neatly crafted fish—so exquisitely rendered,
perhaps the maker's mark is hidden on its belly, beneath
the slivered silver of its shiny scales.

ASSISTED LIVING

Wandering through the door
of my grandmother's room, a woman
leans close to her and asks,

Have you seen Rose?

Thin as a sapling, robe
gaped open, revealing
bruised and mottled skin—

her eyes beseech, hands
wringing as if she were God
re-creating Rose

from a rib of air. Grandmother says *no,*
we're sorry—and the woman walks
out, moaning the way

the wind moans when it whips
around a house, rattling windows,
searching for cracks.

A Day in the Life

Shuffling around the house
in a pair of tattered blue

slippers, wearing a bathrobe,
prescription sunglasses,

and Velcro rollers in my gray-
streaked hair, I feel like some

demented old tart, gearing up
for an afternoon of soaps.

All I need is a T.V. tray,
four or five screeching cats

and a stack of hairdo magazines
to complete this "stage set"

of life on the flip side of forty,
a tragicomedy unfolding

in my living room. I used to use
fewer props, as I recall, jumping

out of bed, sleek as an otter,
sliding down the day, squealing—

but times have changed. Now I
need at least two hours to trowel

on makeup, spray gunk in my
hair, find clothes that won't

pinch, pick or otherwise annoy me,
pack my purse, plaster a smile

on my gravity-challenged face
and greet the morning before

it knocks on my door like one
of those perky cosmetic-

hawking neighbors, handing out
pink sample sacks of futility.

GRANNY SAID

Granny said *turn your ring around*
when a black cat crossed the road
and then the baby died. A neighbor
dosed him with castor oil and that

was the end of Clyde Willis White,
three months old. Papa made his little

coffin with his own hands and Granny
near lost her mind with grief. She
carried on so long, Papa moved

them to the city. Granny took one
look and said *Law, I never seen
so many roads going every which way,
and black cats waiting to cross.*

SEVENTEEN

Somehow you never meet the boys
Who drive convertibles, the ones who breeze
By you on the highway, doing at least eighty—
Blond hair rippling like fields of ripe wheat.
You imagine them pulling into long driveways
Leading to houses often featured
In glossy magazines, with swimming
Pools, gazebos and garage apartments
For the family chauffeur.

Instead, you meet your best friend's pimply
Brother, who wears black stretch socks
With open-toed sandals and sets the cruise control
On his dad's sedan ten miles below the speed limit.
He keeps a five-dollar bill pinned inside
The waist band of his pants for emergencies,
And buys you a wrist corsage from Wal-Mart
A week before the prom—a pale orchid
With brown spots forming near the edges.

So you close your eyes for the first slow dance,
Imagine your head on a different shoulder, broader,
More solid—his wind-whipped hair just grazing
The collar of a single-breasted dinner jacket.
He whispers a line of Rilke in your ear, tells you
That you are all the gardens he has ever gazed at,
Longing—not how he's decided for sure,
To attend community college since
It's so much cheaper and closer to home.

EMPTY

In Grandmother's house, nothing
moves the stagnant air. Not a page turns
nor a cup lifts from its matching saucer.
Curtains hang limp and yellowed

over a rust-ringed sink. The idle blades
of ceiling fans are covered in dust. Pillows
imprinted with human shapes lie
un-plumped in chairs.

Doors remain ajar or shut, never changing;
the hands of clocks are still, inside
their cases. The broom that swept the walk
stands silent in the corner.

Towels that wiped the plates and mitts
that grasped the pots are stacked in drawers
that never open. Numbers never dialed
sit by the phone.

Like mollusk shells, abandoned on a beach,
these rooms are empty—empty as ballet
shoes without a dancer's feet, empty
as this house without her in it.

JUBAL TANNER

They called Jubal Tanner a hard man.
He built a fence around his farm
and didn't take to neighbors leaning
over it. He drove a battered pickup truck
to town once a month, packed it full
of canned goods and chickenfeed,
and went home without so much
as a nod to passersby.

His funeral lasted five minutes
and had two mourners, one of them
the preacher.

Shocked to see that Jubal had no
friends, his brother said, "Why,
he could dance and do card tricks,
tell a story like nobody's business.
Never took a drink in his life,"
he added, leaning

against the local bar. "He was
a good man, a kind man—loved
his family more than anything,
especially that boy of his."

Jubal Tanner married? A father?
"Never in this world," said the people
gathered around. "Not him."

"He was," said his brother, "but they
died some years back—tore him up
something terrible, as I recall." Then he
downed his drink, left a two-dollar tip
and made his way fast, through
the muttering crowd. It was a hard
town—and he couldn't wait
to leave it.

II

Sleeping Alone

I hate to sleep alone.
The bed looks

like Antarctica, cold
and white.

There's no one
around for miles.

Every sound
is magnified—

ice tumbling
in the freezer,

the wind bashing
its fist against

the window, the drip,
drip, of a leaky

faucet. If only I
could mold my

body to your
familiar shape,

breathe you in,
like anesthesia.

TOMATO SANDWICH

Leaning on the counter
by an open window
with tomato juice dripping down
your chin and mayonnaise
gathering

in the corners of your mouth
as soggy, white bread
sticks to your teeth

and your tongue tingles

from the tangy taste of salt
and pellets of fresh
ground pepper burn the back

of your throat, you can't help
but think that eating
a garden tomato sandwich
in your own kitchen is finer
than a café lunch
in Paris.

SUN BATH

Mama told me to play in the house a while,
and I knew what that meant. My baby brother
had some kind of red rash all over his body
and the doctor said sunlight would cure it.
So, my mother stripped him naked and laid
him on a blanket in the backyard every morning
for a week, which must have worked fine
since that rash went away and never came back.
It seemed silly for me to stay indoors when he
was just a baby and I'd seen him sitting
in the bathtub about a billion times, but my
mother clearly thought it was disrespectful
for me to be gallivanting around the yard
with him lying out there, uncovered. I did
watch from a window once, not that I wanted
to see what he looked like since I already
knew that, but because I wasn't supposed
to peek, which is a powerful incentive.
What I noticed first were my brother's fat legs,
and I have to say, they were the fattest
legs in the world, with dimpled flesh
packed on the bone like bread dough rising
from a pan. Mama kissed and made over
those rolls of fat like he was the most beautiful
baby God ever made, which of course, he
wasn't. That would have been me. Anyway,
I saw my brother's bare legs kicking the air,
my mother close beside him on that blanket—
her head propped on one hand, her other hand
making these strange motions over his body.

If I had to say what she was doing, it looked
like she was pouring light over his skin,
one palm-full at a time. It made my eyes
sting and throat burn like fire, watching
the two of them together—him naked
as a newborn, her gathering his share
of sunlight and anointing him with it, over
and over again—not that I was jealous,
although I was perfectly capable of it, but
even a little sinner like me recognized pure
love when it was staring her right in the face.

The Singing of Birds

*(for my great-great grandmother, Mary
Edwards, who bled to death at 49)*

**Rise up, my love, my fair one, and come
away. For, lo, the winter is past, the rain
is over and gone; The flowers appear on
the earth; the time of the singing of birds
has come...Song of Solomon, 2:10-12**

"Oh Law, it's all rushing by
me like a river roar—how we lay
down by the loblolly tree

and you whispered them sweet
things in my ear. I swannee, I never
heard such," she said, on the tenth

day of bleeding. "After that, we
kept having young'uns. I never

dreamed we'd have so many.
Is that you, Laura?" she said,

peering into the corner. "Where'd
your daddy go, child? I can't
hardly move under all these covers.

Seems like my legs are weighted
down by water—and them birds
outside are singing up a storm."

I don't hear any birds, Mama.
The window's shut tight.

"Well, then, you best fetch your
daddy. Tell him the birds are
singing. Tell him I said, come."

DAISY CHAIN

As if the swell of this woman's hips
were mounds of rich, dark earth,
children bloomed from her body
like daisies—

four little girls, all blonde,
each of them touching her somehow—
a hand, a shoulder, something,

while she stood on the side
of the road, talking to neighbors.

Perhaps a sense of danger kept them
huddled close—cars rounding
the curve, drivers staring. In our
defense, it isn't every day we pass
a scene like this: belonging so
palpable, it beat like a heart
on the pavement.

MARCIE CULPEPPER

Miss Marcie Culpepper loved Sundays better
than any other day because she got up early
and had her breakfast, two blueberry bagels
and a glass of fresh-squeezed orange juice, while
the birds outside her window hunted and pecked
for the best seeds in the feeder, which she liked
watching better than any television show.

Then she'd wash her dishes since she never
could stand a dirty kitchen, and head upstairs
to choose which dress she wanted to wear to church.
She was partial to blue because it played up her
eyes, but she was in a yellow mood since it
was spring and the daffodils were blooming
on the front lawn, pretty as pats of butter

on homemade biscuits. So, she picked the one
with the paisley print and Peter Pan collar that
was just a teeny bit too tight in the waist, but she
could wear it with a light sweater so nobody
would notice. She combed out the curls that were
the envy of every girl in grade school and had
driven her crazy for sixty-seven years. Then

she stepped into a pair of tan low-heeled shoes
she bought last summer on Senior Citizens' Day
at the mini-mall. She packed her purse with tissues,
peppermint gum and a number two pencil in case

the preacher said anything worth writing down,
which he usually didn't, but you never know
and her memory wasn't what it used to be.

After making sure the stove was off and the house
locked, she walked to her car and drove three
blocks to the Methodist Church where her friend,
Ursula, was saving her a seat in the fifth pew from
the front, the same place they always sat. She hoped
the sermon wasn't going to be about the Prodigal Son
again because she was sick to death of that story,

happy as she was for the father and all. She wished
the preacher would talk about great women in the Bible
for a change since there were plenty of them, like Ruth
who says to her mother-in-law, "Your people will
be my people and your God my God," which about
made her cry every time she read it. But wouldn't
you know, she said to herself after squeezing in

beside Ursula and opening the bulletin, he had more
to say about the Prodigal Son. She didn't see how
that preacher was going to wring another sermon
out of those dog-eared pages, but she reckoned that son
of his who left home for Hollywood on a Good Friday
some five years ago had something to do with his
fixation on this particular piece of scripture. Lord

knows what he was getting into out there, although
she did see him in a toothpaste commercial once,
which didn't surprise her since that boy had the nicest
teeth she ever saw that weren't custom-made. Marcie

made a mental note to pray for him later on, after she
and Ursula went to lunch at the *Kopper Kettle*,
where they always ordered shrimp and grits. She

ought to have the diet plate seeing as how her yellow
dress was even tighter than it was the last time she
wore it, but you only live once and there's nothing
in the Bible that says you can't enjoy yourself as long
as you use the good sense God gave you. She didn't
know why some people seemed to think that Christians
ought to spend every waking minute either shoring up

their own salvation or trying to convert the heathen.
Frankly, there weren't any heathen in her neighborhood,
and she only drove so far these days, what with the price
of gas and all. Anyway, you have to take a day off
sometime and as far as she was concerned, not to mention
what it says right there in Exodus about working on
the Sabbath—Sunday was a fine day to do it.

GRANDDADDY'S GHOST

I was thirteen when my grandfather
dropped dead at his cousin's
house in Florida. He was eating a bowl of cereal
and collapsed, face-first,
into the milk. Mama

was stirring a pot of beans
when she took the call. Her knees hit the floor,
loud as gunshots. "Not my daddy,"
she screamed, over and over again

for what seemed like days—until the beans
boiled dry and smoke billowed
around the room like Granddaddy's ghost,
as if he heard his little girl
cry and came running.

MADELINE PARMENTER

Mrs. Madeline Parmenter walked with her head held
high despite being the wife of a drunk in a town
small enough to notice. She took the short, shallow

breaths of a woman wearing a whalebone corset
and seldom spoke—afraid her thoughts would tumble
out like acrobats, once she opened her mouth.

Due to the capricious nature of her husband's moods,
she never invited company to the house, and they
had no friends. So far, he managed to keep a steady

job because it's tough to buy booze without a salary—
but Madeline hadn't worked in years as her
concentration waxed and waned, depending on what

happened at home the night before. Her husband
was never violent—used words instead, like X-Acto
knives, cutting her into confetti-sized pieces.

She was often seen watching the road from her living
room window, her face pinched as pie crust—
waiting for the cavalry, some said, without a shred

of hope they'd get there in time. The neighbors felt
sorry for her, *but what can we do when people won't help
themselves? She ought to leave him before it's too late*

to find another husband, they whispered, as if Madeline
Parmenter would ever place her tender psyche in any
man's hands again, over her cold, dead body.

SEPTEMBER IN THE SOUTH

After the summer soup of July
and August, when the air is thick
and muggy and rises from the ground
like hot smoke, September brings

the promise of relief. The miasma
of heat enveloping your house
at daybreak no longer lingers.
Nights stop marinating

your body in its bed like steak
in soy sauce. The terrarium feel

of standing in your own living room
disappears, and light shines bright
and clear as a toddler's gaze through

every pane of glass. You can take walks
without wading through humidity, sit

for hours on the front porch, watching
shadows lengthen. But all too soon,

the evening breeze carries the first brisk
breath of autumn. The scent
of blooming magnolias gives way

to burning leaves and baked apples—
and suddenly, September is gone,
like a beautiful woman lost in a crowd,
before you can call out her name.

TIME

One time, I looked away.
It was less than a second,
faster than two beats
of a hummingbird's wing,
and you were gone. I
screamed your name—
ran like a rabbit, zigzagging
the neighborhood—terror hot
and thick as tar oozing
down my throat, hardening
in my stomach. A hundred
years later, I found you at
the playground. You were
laughing, your feet so high
in the air, God could have
grabbed you easily, by your
loose sandal. Instead, it
was me pulling you off
the swing, my arms holding
you so tight, you came out
the other side of me, grown.

ILA'S GARDEN

Ila kept a small garden where she'd kneel,
of a morning, in homage to the flowers there.
The sun shone hard on her head, but her wide-
brimmed straw hat was tightly woven, its ribbons
tied around her chin in a neat bow.

Undaunted by a trove of tools with masculine
names—trowel, shovel, rake—she worked the rich,
red earth, her manicured nails scrubbed clean

as new pots and coated with clear polish, safely
wrapped inside a pair of cotton gloves. She
peeled brittle containers from the tender

roots of plants and placed them in the beds
she'd made, tucked blankets of soil beneath their
leafy chins. Then she stood, tamed a wayward

curl, and surveyed her achievement. From
the great height of her less-than-five-foot frame,
her garden was a marvel: flowers doffing pink

caps of petals when the wind strolled by, their
sweet scent wafting through the air and into the open
windows of her bedroom. Smiling with satisfaction,

Ila rinsed her tools and stored them in their proper
places, hung her hat on a hook by the back door
like she had done for decades. She put water

on the stove to boil, spooned coffee into a rose-
patterned cup. Then she sat a while, after that,
on the screened-in porch—watching her memory's
waltz, the dip and sway of all the hours,
slowly turning.

SALESMAN

Maybe death is like a door-to-door salesman.
Not the eager boy with the spit-shined shoes,
but a middle-aged man in a brown Derby
hat. His tie is egg-stained and crooked,
shirt frayed at the cuffs. Streaks of dust
cover his worn-out loafers, lucky pennies
lost on the road. He carries a battered
briefcase. You know it's empty as soon
as he sits down, smiles at you from across
the room—a sad smile, filled with regret.
You lament the curlers in your hair
or the grass-stained jeans, hastily pulled
on when the doorbell rang. Had you known
he was coming, you would have dressed
better. You offer him a cup of coffee
in hopes he might stay a while, delaying
the inevitable. He declines, politely,
and stands up. Taking note of how tired
he looks, face droopy and creased as an old
hound dog's, you feel kind of sorry for him,
for what he's there to do, but sorrier
for yourself—unless you're very sick
or in pain. Then you might be ready—
relieved, in fact, which makes it easier
on both of you. But don't feel bad. Most
people squirm in their chairs, consider
making a run for it, as if it would do them
any good to run. Or regret opening
the door in the first place. He might have
moved on then, to another house. You tell
yourself this, but you know better, don't you?

Delta Blues

You're sitting at a bar, sucking up
smoke from cheap cigars and unfiltered
cigarettes in a room-full of drunks
and ramblers, good-time girls

and grifters. From a makeshift stage,
a wizened old guitar picker drops

blue notes into your head like quarters
in your own personal juke box.
His calloused fingers fly across

the frets, soaking that wood with every
drop of sorrow he's ever known.

Seems like a man should roll a stone
over hurt that deep, but here he is,
lifting it up like Lazarus for anybody
lucky enough to listen.

FANNIE

When Fannie fell down
the stairs, everyone laughed.
She wasn't hurt, after all,
and besides, it was Fannie—
the girl with the pea head
and stringy hair that stopped
just short of her big ears,
and that voice of hers,
like a squeaky cartoon.
And talk about clumsy.
She was always tripping
over her own shoestrings
or flopping in a chair so hard,
it skidded across the floor.
It was death to be seen
anywhere near her because
somebody might say, *she's*
FRIENDS with Fannie, which
was worse than wearing
a nightgown to school
or throwing up in class.
But one sunny afternoon,
we walked outside for recess
and Fannie sidled up to me,
slipped her hand in mine.
And because I didn't shake it
off like a spider or scream
in horror, I got my first crack
at feeling noble. It was Fannie,
however, who deserved the gold
star I gave myself for it.

PAPA NEVER LEARNED TO READ

Granny sat under a shade tree,
fanning herself with corn shucks,

while Papa stood waist-deep in

the river, baptizing. Folks rose up,
sputtering, and waded back to shore—

their sodden dresses and pant legs

heavy against their skin, their souls
light as Easter lilies. "I see no need

for such as that," Granny said, to

anyone who asked. Still, she read
Papa scripture—the words warmed

by her breath and scattered into his

brain like dandelion seeds—where
once a week, they grew into a sermon.

III

The Speckled Trout Café

He was having the Paul Tate Special with a glass
of Gnarly Head Old Vine Zinfandel at the Speckled
Trout Café & Oyster Bar when she walked in
and ruined everything. When you can't even eat
a decent meal without being bedazzled by some
red-headed woman sitting under a fern basket, you
might as well stay home. She took her time
with the menu, finally ordering Scallop and Shrimp
Almerindo—his second favorite dish at his favorite
restaurant, proving she had good taste in food
if not in clothes. The color of her blouse clashed
with her hair, and a hit of helium under that circus tent
of a skirt would probably send her up to Pluto, (which
was no longer a planet, according to yesterday's
paper). Well, he wasn't falling for any such charms
as a wide-eyed stare in his direction and that half-
moon dimple cutting into her right cheek when she
smiled—something she seemed to do most of the time.
He'd had enough of women, especially good lookers
who seldom lived up to the promise of their beauty.
There she goes again, smiling at me proper this time,
he thought—an invitation if he ever saw one. But
before he could grab his wine glass and join her,
which he had every intention of doing despite any
misgivings to the contrary, a guy who had to be
younger than his best pair of boots beat him
to it. She looked delighted out of her skull when
that boy pulled up a chair, meaning he'd misread
the situation. Despairing of the whole business
of men and women and their foolish goings-on,
he dug into his Paul Tate Special with the attention
he should have paid to it in the first place.

LAUNDROMAT

In the lint-filled, fabric-softened air
of the Laundromat, we listened
to the whoosh of washing machines
as they filled with water and churned

dirty clothes and the thump, thump
of dryers with metal snaps and buttons
clicking against the drum, while we
munched on vending machine peanuts

until our mouths puckered with salt.
Clothes hitting dryer glass windows
made rows of kaleidoscopic color
as washers wobbled and walked across

the floor, and mothers carrying baskets
kept filing in and filing out, kids
following close behind them like baby
chicks. There weren't many men

doing laundry in those days, except
the poor souls who had no women in
their lives. Husbands saw neatly folded
clothes appear out-of-nowhere in their

cedar-scented drawers, while wives
and children, the smell of powdered
detergent still clinging to our skins,
knew exactly where they came from.

TRUMPETER SWAN

From the cobwebbed
mist hovering
over the lake,
a trumpeter swan
calls to his mate,
the sound
sonorous
and haunting.
Wanting
the feathered
curve of her
white neck,
the soft breast
of her against
his own, he waits,
wings quivering.
I long for you,
like this.

New Orleans

Sunlight flowed in yolk-yellow streams
down Canal Street, where an ancient black man spewed
rhythm and blues from a Selmer saxophone. Notes
sailed through the shrimp and piss-scented air

like frangipani petals scattered over an old bawd, sleeping
off a drunk. They bounced off cigarette butts, beer

cans and glistening gobs of freshly-hawked spit,
through the walls of every building on the block,
easy as ghosts on roller skates. With lungs like a pearl

diver, he played all day as crowds strolled
by or lingered, tossing crumpled bills and pocket change

into the satin center of a brown bowler hat. Tourists
tapped their feet to the zippy tunes and turned melancholy
when the music dripped slower

than maple syrup over some sad mental pancake
they'd never eat again. Just before dark,

he packed his sax in a velvet-lined case and whistled
his way home, where he folded his withered
body into a tub of soapy water with a finger of gin

on the side, and watched the same film that ran
through his head night after night—

the one where a girl named Maja-Lisa, long gone,
beckoned him to the bedroom with her orchid-soft hands,
where her sighs and moans mingled with sounds

from an open window: cats fighting over fish bones,
bums snoring in the alley, hookers culling clients

from snickering herds of college boys. Maybe he'd write
that song down sometime and call it, "New Orleans,"
but probably not, he thought, the smooth taste
of liquor only half as sweet as Maja-Lisa's mouth.

Another Memory of My Mother's Kindness

At the end of our street
was a small patch of land
where a neighbor's
grandfather, his body bent
as a boomerang, tilled
the ground and planted seeds.
At harvest time, the sun
beat down hard as rain
and mottled his bare back,
cupped like a hand over rich
swells of dirt and the foliate
flare of ripe cabbages.
Come noon, he'd lean against
a shade tree and drink
the tall glass of lemonade
my mother always brought
him, sowing seeds of her
own while we watched—
and remembered.

BETTY'S ROADSIDE DINER

Unaware of its anachronistic status,
Betty's Roadside Diner with its rusty sign blinking,
stands between mile markers
on a desert highway. Like a blazing

campfire to a cluster of tired cowboys, the diner,
with its dazzling lights, lures
lonely drifters and famished families,
road-weary truckers and the down
and out. You can still get a piece of fruit pie
for a dollar fifty and free re-fills
on coffee, and somebody's

sure to say hello when you walk in.
The waitresses look like sisters, with lined
faces and chiseled cheekbones,
their hair (the color of mud flats

or dust bunnies) laminated with generous
layers of hairspray. They wait patiently,
(holding tiny lead pencils), to write
down your culinary pleasure
while the greasy air coats

your lungs slick as corn oil
in a cast-iron skillet. The fry-cook scrapes
a metal spatula over an open griddle,

dividing heaping mounds of hash brown
potatoes into separate servings
and scooping them into plates

that rattle on the countertop every time
a big rig rumbles by.

Florescent tubes that line
the ceiling are so bright, you can see your own
soul through the backs of your hands,
(though it doesn't seem to bother babies,

curled in corner booths like cocktail shrimps,
dreaming the night away). There's a sense
of isolation surrounding everyone,

as if they're actors in separate plays—
yet it comforts you to see them. In fact,

it seems like all that's warm and safe
in the whole world lies amid the fake leather seats
and unfamiliar faces of folks who wound
up here tonight, in the same place as you.

Stairway
to Heaven

(for my brother)

The middle sofa
cushion worked
best, with its two
stiff wedges
of stuffed fabric.
You could brace
both your feet
instead of one,
which skewed
the trajectory
down the long
flight of stairs.
Then you went
sort of sideways
and sometimes
fell off, prematurely.
So, we took turns
with the good
cushion, although
occasionally risked
a single-stirrup ride.
We might have
broken our necks,
of course, but never
did. You waited
a few years to die,
not many—while
I live on and on,
breaking in ways
we never imagined.

BLUE HYDRANGEAS

I know it sounds strange, but them blue hydrangeas
saved me, she said, staring out the window. He sat
right there, where you are now—in that very same
chair. He was kindly leaning forward as I recall,
his hands flying through the air like white doves
tethered to a string. I could see his lips moving,
but what I heard was the wind rustling through
the leaves and what I felt were petals on my cheek,
the cool blue of them soaking into my skin like rain.
And nothing he said hurt me one bit, not even the part
about how he didn't love me anymore, which he
must have meant since he packed his bags and left.
I might have lost my mind with grief, I loved him
so, but them blue hydrangeas bloomed all summer,
like they were friends of mine who wouldn't leave
my side for a minute. And then one morning, I tried
to conjure up his face and couldn't do it. To this
day, when I think of him, all I see is blue.

MADISON'S PICTURE

In Madison's picture, I am smiling.
My hair is long and flying out,

like a dog's ears from the window
of a car, zooming down a highway.

With arms wide open, I have a bright
red apple in one hand and a blue

balloon in the other. There is a yellow
bird with an orange beak perched

on my hip, and I am wearing pink
shoes, my toes pointed, like a ballerina.

Green grass grows beneath me, but my feet
don't touch the ground, as if she drew

me in mid-jump. There is a flower
with ten purple petals, and a round,

yellow sun in the corner of the page,
with a single ray touching my outstretched

hand, (the one holding an apple).
It seems she captured me, with her box

of crayons and earnest concentration,
on the happiest, best day I ever had,

and gave it back to me as a gift—
even better than I remembered.

SQUIRREL

Gray little glutton,
his tail twitching
like a trigger-finger,

empties my feeder
tray faster than
a vacuum cleaner.

Jaws jam-packed
with bird seed,
husks hanging

from his whiskers,
he leaps across
the lawn and up

a tree, the swag
of his fat belly
flaking bark.

Brunson Elementary School
(1964)

With the heater blowing full-blast
and rain dripping down the windows in strange
rivulets that veered left or right according

to some rule of water, and my mother
with her clean, young face and strong hands
gripping the steering wheel with such

ferocity, and all the little ducklings in their
yellow slickers and rubber galoshes trudging
up the wet walkway towards their chalk-

scented, fluorescent-lighted classrooms
where ruby-lipped strangers waited with their
beehive hair-dos and shiny shoes, (who

might not cut the crusts off sandwich bread
or feel our heads for fever), I thought
perhaps I wouldn't go to first grade, after

all. But the car door opened as if by magic,
though it must have been my own small
set of fingers pulling up the handle.

ROCKY'S IRISH SETTER

Maggie was a gypsy,
her fleet-footed body a flame-red
caravan, always on the move.

She spent her days outdoors—
a streak of fire racing
through the woods and fields,

or rolling on her back, paws
waving, ears flung
like nets from a boat, trolling

the air for sounds. Her thick coat
gathered burrs and sticks,
the scent of wild mushrooms,

the musk of cats—which her master
washed away in the evenings,
his hands gentle,

his voice softer than fresh-mown
lawns, softer than warm
blankets, softer than anything.

WIDOW LANE

A whiskey jug lamp
sits on a red dresser
in the hallway.

It's never dark
there with the lamp lit,
so Evelyn finds

her way, easily,
to the bedroom. She
sleeps between

sachet-scented
sheets—her slippers
tucked away,

collapsed and empty
as used boxes.
She dreams

of cable cars
and picnics, her flirty
sister who married

young and never
learned to drive.
Evelyn liked boys

better in groups,
but finally picked one,
under pressure.

He owned a fancy
car and hated
her mother,

who poisoned
their marriage faster
than arsenic

in a well. Now
she lives alone
on a dead-end street

that sags
with the weight
of widows,

their sighs heavy
as furniture,
their faces

framed like portraits,
peering from
every window.

SAVING GRACE

Oh, the hard hours in a day that seem
to gather like wind, a cyclone spinning on fear—

the unpaid bills; the aches and pains; the perpetual fretting over
one thing and another. So I begin each morning simply.

There is the measuring and mixing, standing by a warm
stove, half asleep. In two minutes I tip

the pot, pour Cream of Wheat into a bowl and carry
it to the table, already set with napkin and spoon. I drop a pat

of butter in the center, pour in a goodly portion
of real maple syrup and stir, inhaling sweet steam, rising.

I sit in the same hard-backed chair in front of a bay
window through which the sun beams, in fine weather,

eating my hot breakfast, slowly—watching
chickadees and cardinals, Carolina wrens and gold finches

feast on a tray filled with sunflower seeds. Whatever
maelstrom follows, first, there is this.

IV

The Coffin Maker

They summoned Papa sometimes, when
someone died after hours. The heavy black phone
would jangle in the hallway,

drag him from the bed where Granny slept,
the frayed rope of her pigtail stretched
across the pillowcase. He'd step into overalls

flecked with wood dust, and a pair
of thick-soled boots—creep down the stairs
to the kitchen. Granny stored leftover

biscuits in the oven so he'd drown a few
in blackstrap molasses and eat them, standing
over the sink. Then he'd climb into his '36 Ford

and drive through the vacant, half-lit streets
to Turner-White Casket Company, an ancient
building covered in tin, with brass

shaded oil lamps dangling from the ceiling.
There, he'd work through the night—making
one more sturdy ark, built to last.

QUEEN'S COURT

Swathed in scarves and rouged
up to her earlobes,
Ethel sat fiddling with double
ropes of pearls,

her fingers worrying those beads
with near-prayerful

reverence. "Doll baby,"
she said to my brother, "give
Aunt Ethel some sugar,"

which he did, while I sat across
the room wondering

why mamas made over boys
like they were something special,
when it was clear
as wedding bells that women

ruled the cosmos like a coterie
of cotillion-christened queens.

Old Holler Church

Beneath the blossom-laden boughs of a wild cherry
tree, ladies in sensible shoes, heavy as hooves,
clutch Bibles and purses close to their flower-festooned
bodices. Pinned like butterflies to their Mother's Day
corsages, they smile or frown, depending upon
the conversation. The women bearing infants
sway to and fro, soothing cranky babies

in the cradles of their arms, while children
in their scuffed Sunday best, race around the churchyard,
capricious as loose leaves caught by the wind. The men
gather like black-fleeced sheep by the church doors,
their jackets shiny with age and use. A few
are solemn and sour-faced, still sucking on the lemon
of this week's sermon,

with all their secret habits labeled "sin." Others grin
and slap each other on the back, secure in their salvation.
Teenagers mill around in separate groups, eyeing
their latest crush or itching to get away from church
and family. What they all know for sure,
unless the Lord calls them home—they'll be back
for Wednesday night potluck supper.

MERRY-GO-ROUND

Oh, the thrill of it, to clasp those wooden
withers with your scrawny
legs, to put your feet in the stirrups while
the carousel slowly turns and children
climb on, clamoring for the best ponies.
There is barely time to notice the fancy

scroll-work on the saddle
and the swirl of painted mane before you're

moving faster and faster, clutching
the shiny silver pole as your horse
goes up and down and the carousel circles
round and round. The air

rushes by, pungent with popcorn
and caramel apples,
elephant ears and cotton candy,
as faces in the crowd
blur and blend. On and on,
your steed surges forward, prancing

to the beat of the band organ, oom pa-pa,
oom pa-pa, until the squeaky sound

of ancient gears grinding to a halt signals
the final turn and strong arms lift
you from your seat as if you're not a cowgirl
riding the range nor an Arabian knight,
but a child who wants to go-round again.

COOL

In a leather jacket, James Dean
kind of way, Tom
slouched through the halls

of Hanes High School,
grinning at girls. He combed
his coal-black ducktail

into a point, his hands moving
around his head
like pomade-scented birds.

Leaning with practiced
nonchalance against assorted
door jams, he waited for Loretta

Wray, the homecoming queen,
to sashay by with her
giggling gang of friends.

She was so beautiful, the knees
of every boy buckled
at the sight of her, so he played

it cool until she married
him—breaking a hundred male
hearts, like glass.

WASHING MY BABY'S HAIR OVER THE KITCHEN SINK

There is the weight of her small, solid head in my hand
and the feel of warm water, sluicing through her hair.
Eyes the soft blue-gray of herons' wings,
follow my new-mother face, glowing.
Enthralled with each other, we
coo like doves in the milk-
scented air that my baby
breathes out and I
breathe
in.

Two Crows

Two crows walked down a wet road,
their heads bobbing like black umbrellas
along a city sidewalk. I envied them their
companionable stroll, the flock that settled
on the grass beside them, when my day
was spent alone, missing you. You
are nowhere and everywhere, the pervading
absence of you more present than this chair,
this desk, the window through which my gaze
moves like a ghost. My thoughts fly
to you like birds through rain-drenched
clouds, or songs through a roof, piercing
the sky like stars—while crows lift up
together, their wings stretched to breaking.

FOLKE, DOWN ON THE FARM

The old Swede sits in a plastic chair, his blue-veined hands
limp in his lap; a wooden cane leaning against one knee. A rooster
crows; a black dog chases a rubber ball again and again,
thrown by whoever bothers to toss it.

With nearly sightless eyes, he stares across a plot of land
planted with spinach and collard greens,
to a distant field. Here, an ex-bush pilot displays his daring moves,
the belly of his plane brushing the tops of trees and looping

upward, towards the clouds. The engine's roar is like a thousand
bees buzzing in jelly jars, yet the old man doesn't hear it.
Perhaps he feels a faint vibration, like echoes of recollection
bouncing from room to room

in his failing memory. Still, he sits there, content—
blue sky stretching canvas-like over his head, a cool breeze
blowing the scant white threads cut close to his scalp. He might
be pondering images left to him from his long,

good life, or simply taking pleasure in the sun's waning warmth.
His profile will remain, however, stamped like a king's face
on newly-minted coins that will jingle in our pockets
years after he is gone.

Pool Day

Greased up and decked out in new bathing suits, plastic sunglasses
and flip-flops, my brother and I waited in line with our mother
at the entrance to Tanglewood Pool, clutching rubber rafts
and over-sized beach towels with neon stripes you could spot
from the moon. The mingled scents of chlorine, coconut suntan lotion
and French fries drenched in tomato ketchup, along with the whoops
of joy and continuous splashing sounds that kids create
when they're cavorting in a pool, was enough to send us into a swoon
of anticipated ecstasy. But there were two metal turnstiles
we had to pass through after Mom paid the baby-faced cashier

with the sun-bleached hair, and signs that read, *Girls to the Left,*
Boys to the Right. Then we had to make our way through the women's
changing room and a gauntlet of naked, squealing toddlers,
grandmas trying to shimmy into too-tight one-piece suits they kept
swearing fit them the year before, stick-thin teenagers in micro-bikinis
examining their faces in a row of cracked mirrors, although what they
were looking for, I couldn't imagine, and that was just the girls'
side. What my brother endured, we never inquired. Finally,
we converged on the sunlit promenade to poolside, while our mother
scoped out available spaces where we could set up camp

for the next four hours. She was easily the best looking woman
there like she always was everywhere she went, but we didn't realize
it at the time. However, we did see a few fathers puffing up
like toads when they caught sight of her, and other mothers peering
at her like she was an alien who landed in a silver spaceship,
possibly searching for husbands to abduct. No doubt accustomed
to such scrutiny, she passed right by them, smooth as a parade float,

73

and we followed, trying our best not to run. The last thing
we wanted was to be singled out by a lifeguard blowing that shrill,
eardrum-popping whistle.

After spreading the towels and unpacking our gear, Mom always added
yet another layer of suntan lotion to our wriggling, impatient bodies,
which back then was about as effective as slathering us with mustard.
We inevitably wound up red as two strips of bacon, shaking
and shivering from what felt like sun poisoning, and every turn
in the sheets that night was skin-pinching agony. A day at the pool,
however, was worth any price, particularly that first ride down
the water slide, which had to be faster than flying—followed
by an icy splash and total submersion into another world, filled
with muffled sounds, fluid motion and puckered feet.

Morning Glories

Morning glories march
on green feet, up
the porch rails.

With purple bugles
blaring, they advance
at dawn.

Their troops
gain ground, inch
by inch, day by day,

until the porch looks
like a float in nature's
victory parade.

A Rancher Buries His Wife

They buried her in sun-baked ground, his wife
of fifty years.

A cowbird whistled from a crucifixion thorn,
and a freight train clacked

down the tracks. He stood apart
from the rest of them—folks whose names he

never cared to know, remembering of all things,
her hair haloed with light,

and the scent of her, still clinging to the clothes
she left behind.

He would die of it, this loneliness.
Already his hands were curling up, his fingers

turning blue. He used to be afraid of death.
Now he'd welcome it, like rain.

DRUID HILL DRIVE

On Druid Hill Drive,
we were laughing, wiggling
flashes
of mismatched clothes

and spindly limbs,
who spun our parents

in circles as we dashed
in and out of assorted kitchens,
the sound of banging
screen doors loud

as canon fire, family dogs
barking like mad

from the porch. With bikes
to ride and trees
to climb, forts to build
and bugs

to catch, there were
barely enough hours

in the day for all the things
we wanted to do before
bedtime, when sleep

grabbed us like an undertow,
dragging tired children

to their weary rest
and back again,
for another round
of summer.

FISHERMAN

A gray-bearded man tossed wading boots
and tackle, fishing rods and reels in the back
of a pick-up truck, and wiped his hands on a trout-
scented rag—scales clinging to the cloth
like glitter on a Christmas card. He shoved it

in the pocket of jeans washed so many times,
they were white as osprey wings and soft

on his skin, just the way he liked them. After
climbing in the driver's seat, he took off down

the road, rocks flying every which way under
his tires and dust rising like it did when he
was a boy, running home to supper. He could

still see his mother divvying up cornbread,
his father gazing at her like she was an angel

who landed, by mistake, in their kitchen. And
come nightfall when they all crawled into bed,

bellies full and bodies worn out from work and play,
he'd drift off to sleep wondering how life could
get any better than this—and sure enough, it hadn't
yet, except for early mornings when the fish were biting
and the sun finally rose, setting the lake on fire.

TRANSACTION

A hooker stood in the parking lot of a Super 8
motel in Marion, North Carolina, talking
on a cell phone. She had dyed blonde hair
and two busted fingers taped together with dirty
bandages, and a pair of black plastic sunglasses
perched on her nose. She was skinny as the grip-end
of a long-handled shovel, wearing a dark shirt,
low-rise jeans and a snakeskin belt.

A car with Virginia plates pulled up and she
stepped close to the driver's side, slipping
her cell phone into a beaded purse hanging off
her bony shoulder. She commenced negotiating
price with a man young enough to be her son,
from the look of his smooth skin and wispy beard,
but plenty old enough to know that cash money
can't cover the cost of every transaction.

V

Cat Head Biscuits

A man slid into a booth at Big Nell's,
the checkered tablecloth strobing
like a bad suit on cable T.V. He ordered
black coffee, three eggs, sunny,

and a cat head biscuit from a waitress
named Doris.

The place filled up fast with rheumy-eyed
old men with sunburned pates,
families of multiple shapes

and sizes, and a group of middle-aged ladies
with straw bags and floppy hats,
sand still clinging

to their painted toenails. The coffee
came first, leaving a bitter taste on his tongue,

but in two shakes he was sopping
up yolks with a hunk of cat head biscuit,
reading a dog-eared flyer on the miraculous
powers of bee pollen.

WHEN THE SKY MAKES LOVE TO YOU

When
the sky
makes love
to you,
it brings

down
its colors—
swags
of gold
and streaks

of lavender,
azure-veined
arms
that wrap
you in

clouds.
It breathes
daybreak
into your
mouth,

telling tales
of dusk
and the fiery
tips of stars,
how it

yearns to lift
you into itself,
and over
the earth
entire.

AULD LANG SYNE

Years ago, families sat outside on a warm day,
in folding chairs set up under a shade tree. The men
would smoke and discuss "the game," occasionally flirting
with the ladies, who talked among themselves (when
they weren't busy hollering at children or pouring

lemonade out of ice-cold pitchers), about recipes
and the latest virus to pass through the house,
how they were tired of wiping noses and wasn't June,
hot as it was, a blessed relief?

Supper was grilled hamburgers on Sunbeam bread
with bags of salty chips and Aunt Nancy's homemade
banana ice cream, sweet as summer afternoons
cooling into dusk, when the bats come out
and night waits like a pool for the day to jump in.

CROCHET LESSON

"Like this," said Anna, her hand guiding mine.
"I'm eighty-two tomorrow, and I've worked
hard all my life. After the war, soldiers came
to my village in Hungary. They took my sister
and me to a camp in Russia. We were there
five years in the coal mines. Sometimes
they marched us into town to buy provisions.
The townspeople hated us, so we had to have
protection—always an armed guard. It isn't
easy being hated, let me tell you. You never get
used to it. Wrap the yarn around your fingers
this way, and it goes easier. In the mines, we used
dynamite to break apart the coal, and it was up
to me to put the sticks into holes and light the fuses.
Once, I had a bad feeling. I told the girls beside
me to get out fast, and then the wall caved in,
right where we were standing. We were lucky
that day. A few months later, I had a hemorrhage,
pushing a cart filled with coal up a steep hill.
There were three of us, but it was still too heavy.
When I started coughing blood, they walked me
to the hospital, an hour away. Four days I stayed
in bed, but it got boring, let me tell you. It is
better to be busy. Look how well you've done,"
she said, smiling. "Another hard worker, like me."

MY FATHER

My father has a set of shapely legs
that beauty queens would envy, from years
of hiking golf courses, hauling clubs
without caddie or cart. He has a farmer's
tan from playing all day in the hot sun,

wearing short-sleeved shirts and shorts,
and socks with fancy golf shoes. His friends
say he's *a good ole boy* for his even
temper and good sportsmanship, always

glad when the other guy plays well. He
jokes a lot and makes people laugh,
though his joints hurt and his field of vision
narrows by the hour. Against all odds, he
can still drive the ball, still make the putt.

When he lost his only son, he didn't shatter
inward, with shards of bitterness cutting him
to pieces, or fly apart, showering others
with broken glass. His private grief showed

in the slump of his shoulders, the slowing
of his gait—because my father is the kind
of man who walks the course, plays the game,
and carries his own burdens, however
heavy, with honor and dignity, inviolate.

SNOWY EGRET

Stark against the marsh
landscape,

a snowy egret moves
in whispers,

a soft sigh over placid
water—then stands

on one leg, the light
a fading backdrop

to her startling
whiteness.

She could be a bride,
unsure,

or an angel fallen—
a convert preparing

for baptism. Or simply
a bird, a snow-white

bird, searching
the shallows for fish.

PAPA FELL OFF THE PORCH

Papa leaned over the porch railing, looking
for our '62 Rambler on its way back from El Paso,
Texas, and pitched head-first in the bushes. Good
thing they lived in the city because the ambulance
got there fast—just about the time we pulled
up to the curb. Men in white coats laid him
on a stretcher, moaning something terrible. God
was probably used to noise from this particular
penitent since Papa was a Primitive Baptist preacher
and they are not quiet church folk by a long

stretch, but He must have paid close attention
that day since nothing came of it but a goose egg
on Papa's crown. It scared us all to pieces
when it happened—especially Granny,
standing there beside him wearing her best cotton
"company" bonnet one minute and all by herself
the next, and my mother, who remembered Papa's
younger days when he charmed birds and squirrels
right out of the trees and hung the moon outside
her bedroom window for a night light.

MORNING

A woman sits on a hotel balcony,
watching the tide go out. A flock
of pelicans, dark against the gray morning
sky, searches for breakfast

just beyond the shoreline, their throats
deep as buckets beneath their long,

fish-scooping beaks. Her husband
sleeps inside the room as he did the night
before, when the full moon cast
its light upon the waves

in phosphorescent kisses. She lifts her cup
and dreams of someone kissing her,

while foam gathers at the water's edge
like Chantilly cream left
on a plate, un-tasted.

SUNDAY DINNER AT GRANDMA'S HOUSE

With a pot of green beans pressure cooking
on the stove, Grandma kneaded dough for yeast rolls,
flour up to her elbows. The chicken looked done,
but it could wait a second since it was slow-frying
in a pan of corn oil. There was pound cake
on the counter, its flaky crust baked a golden
shade of brown, and fresh peaches piled in a bowl
beside the peeler. It was warm

inside and out, so the back of her neck
was sopping wet despite the fan on the floor
and all the windows raised high, trying to catch a breeze.
They'll be here any minute, she thought, their voices
filling the house like bread batter, rising—
probably half-starved and ready to eat as soon
as they walked in. She was ready, too,
once she popped the rolls

in the oven, put the chicken on paper towels
to drain, checked the beans and finished setting the table.
Of course, she still had to find that nice coral lipstick
that went so well with her beach tan, run a comb
through her hair and hang up her apron. Then she'd
meet us on the front porch, face flushed,
arms wide open, the smell of home cooking
clinging to her skin like perfume.

LILACS

(for Leonard)

While you waited by your father's
death bed, a warbler sang its heart out, and a patch
of clouds, white as glaciers,

drifted over the house. The men in dark suits
came to take his body—asked you to lift his head.
How heavy he must have been,

but you made him seem as light as flowers,
as if you were a small boy holding
lilacs, careful not to crush them in your hands.

WATERMELON SLIM

Somewhere out there, Watermelon Slim
is working a juke joint, easy as a slide. Smoke
swirls around the room like mist off

a swamp—in dimly-lit corners where sugar daddies
chomp on cigars, women pale as napkins
draped over their laps;

above the heads of cowboys tapping
their steel-toed boots,

young girls swaying on the dance floor—
eyes closed—hip bones close to punching holes
in their skin-tight jeans,

middle-aged mamas bumping and grinding
their booze-addled husbands,

and blue-collar workers sitting so still at their
scarred-up tables, cigarettes burn to ash
between their fingertips.

They're all listening hard to this craggy-faced,
truck driving melon picker, his riffs moving

through their heads like slow-roving sidewinders—
hungry for the next spoon-full of ain't got
nobody, baby done left me blues.

GOLDEN YEARS

In a yellow housecoat with metal snaps
and a side-pocket-full of crumpled-up tissues,
she crossed the yard and checked the mailbox
like she always did in the late afternoon.

It was stuffed with the usual junk—doctor bills,
medical supply advertisements and granite
memorial brochures, as if she cared what
they said about her when she was gone. Let
her son in Topeka handle all that, assuming

he knew her name, at least. He was a sweet
boy when he was little, though, and motherhood
was good while it lasted. No use crying over spilt
milk, her daddy always said—words to live by.

She stood there a while, watching cars blow
past and the frantic migration of squirrels
from one side of the road to the other. Just
like people, they wanted to be where they
weren't, even if it killed them. Thank

God she was content with what she had
and where she had it, and for His bountiful
mercy in giving her this old lady suit so she
could do what she damn well pleased.

DEVOTION

Every morning,
a nurse wheeled
Papa into Granny's room,

where he'd sit by her bed
until evening. Granny
just lay there, propped

up on pillows, wearing
a nightgown and bed jacket,

her gray braids tied
with rubber bands.

She kept a pinch of snuff
between her gum

and jaw, and a tissue
wadded in her palm
to wipe her chin.
They didn't say much,

with five or six
strokes between them,

but he'd smooth
her covers sometimes
with shaky hands,
and she would watch

him sleep, nodding
in his chair.

Let young love write
songs—words that blare
from rigged speakers

in souped-up cars,
pounding your eardrums

like swings from a mallet.
Old love is a slow
dance to silence.

Oak Tree

Leaning over a farmhouse where the same
family has lived for generations,
stands an old oak tree: leaves flapping

harder than wind-blown housecoats hung
on a clothesline—roots rummaging
under the porch for a comfortable pair

of shoes. It spends the days basking
in sunlight, or catching raindrops in each
green palm. In winter, its bare limbs tap, tap

against the darkening sky as it waits
impatiently for snow—its boughs like empty
cradles, rocking. It beckons men

and women from the fields in the evenings,
with branches waving like their mothers used
to do when it was time for supper. And

it comforts them to know that year after year,
this ancient oak keeps watch outside their
little farmhouse, its arms spread wide

over their comings and goings, their weddings
and funerals, births and baptisms, firmly
anchored in the hallowed ground of home.

THE BELLE OF BOURBON STREET

She wore a purple feathered boa wrapped
around her shoulders and shoes so high,
the heels looked like a pair of stilts,
and that walk, well it was more like a sashay
with attitude so crowds on Bourbon Street
parted like she was God's hand on the Red Sea
when she passed by. The scent of her perfume
mingled with beignets and chicory coffee
and flowers lush as pregnant Tahitian
princesses. Chlotilde could work

a sidewalk, no doubt about it, and when
she strolled into a bar, the doors opened
like magic as the sound of clinking glasses
and near hysterical laughter and the crack
of a cue ball on the break spilled into the street.
Every stool had her name on it so before
she sat down, the bartender parked
a Tanqueray and tonic with a chilled lime
twist on a crystal coaster. She smiled,
thanked him, and raised "just what

the doctor ordered" to her lips while
every man in the room stopped what he
was doing and watched. Hours later, when
the bar closed down and Chlotilde's
head was resting on her forearm, the bartender
placed a quiet call to the Garden District.
Fifteen minutes on the button a black Rolls
Royce slid along the curb quiet as a cat

in a cathedral and out stepped a big man
in a dinner jacket, his hair a gleaming halo

of silver. What few stragglers were left
knew better than to meet his eye when he walked
past. He put his hand on her back, and asked
the bartender, "She get into trouble Batiste?"
and the bartender shook his head, "No sir,
Mr. Rabalais, it was a good night," which
he didn't argue with although a good
night would be the one where his daughter
stayed sober. He lifted her like he'd done
a thousand times and carried her outside,

that feather boa dragging behind them
like the tail of a comet. "Daddy,"
she murmured, her arms tightening around
his neck. "Yes, Bebé, we goin' home now,"
he said, as he laid her in the back seat—
a gardenia in a corsage box. After
the car disappeared into a patch of fog
rolling in from the river, a young man
on the corner bowed and bid a silent
farewell to the Belle of Bourbon Street.

PERSONAL ACKNOWLEDGMENTS

As ever, I am humbled and grateful for God's everlasting love and inexhaustible supply of patience and forgiveness.

Special thanks to my husband, Leonard, for the many sacrifices you make so that I can live my dreams. Thank you, also, for reading every edition of all my poems, despite your preference for technical manuals—and for schlepping me all over the country. I couldn't do this without you.

To my parents, Tom and Loretta Kirby, my daughter, Gia, future son-in-law, Matt, and my uncle, artist Stephen White, who did the gorgeous painting on the cover of this book—my eternal love and gratitude.

I'd like to acknowledge family and friends who are no longer with us, for inspiring various poems in this collection: Samuel and Nannie Edwards White (Papa and Granny); John Alvin and Ila Evelyn White; John Henry, Sr. and Blanche Fogleman Kirby; Nancy Kirby Ward; Ethel White Linville Flynn; Mary Evelyn Gardner Edwards; Laura Edwards; Folke Erickson; Angeline Carmella Myers; Ursula Beck; Kathleen Bishop (for her incredible butter mints); and of course, Rocky Lugo's beautiful Irish Setter, Maggie.

Love and thanks to Susan Nagel-Bloch, Lisa Hooper, Debra Hardiman, Fran Kiger, Joan Nichols, Art Nadelman, Mick Scott, Phil Montemayor, Maricam Kaleel, Harriet Strickland, Mark C. Houston, Janet Malliett, Yong Tang, Ron Repique, Frances Dunn, Debbie Kincaid, Charity Smosna, Carolyn Hooper, M. Gene Bond, Stella Gibson, Nelson Adams, Tim Plowman and John Beck—to Anna Tumpek Ries, for the "Crochet Lesson" and Madison, for "Madison's Picture,"—and to dear, departed friends, Vickie Johnson, Robert M. Kerr and Narcille Mayeux.

To Kevin Watson of Press 53, for believing in my work, and to all you readers out there, whose support means so much.

And finally, to my "little" brother, Thomas (*Tommy*) M. Kirby, Jr., 1959-1980. I miss you every day.

Terri Kirby Erickson was born in North Carolina, where she has lived most of her life. In addition to traveling extensively, she also lived in Louisiana, Virginia and Texas. Her first collection of poetry is entitled, *Thread Count*. Her work has appeared or is forthcoming in *Basilica Review*, *Bay Leaves*, *Blue Fifth Review*, *Broad River Review*, *Christian Science Monitor*, *Dead Mule*, *Forsyth Woman*, JAMA, *Long Story Short*, *Muse India*, *Parent:Wise Austin*, *Paris Voice*, *Pinesong*, *Pisgah Review*, *Smoking Poet*, *Thieves Jargon*, *Wild Goose Poetry Review*, *Voices and Vision*, and others. The Northwest Cultural Council selected her work in 2006 and 2007 for an international juried poetry exhibit, and her poem, "Oak Tree," received a 2009 *Best of the Net* nomination. Terri lives in Lewisville, NC, with her husband, Leonard, and about a hundred cardboard boxes that their beloved daughter left behind when she grew up and moved out—mostly filled with stuffed animals and shoes.

ABOUT THE COVER ARTIST

STEPHEN WHITE is an artist with a gallery called "Stephen White Graphics" in Carrboro, North Carolina. He specializes in figurative paintings done on wood, in gold leaf and transparent oil glazes.

LaVergne, TN USA
04 May 2010

181498LV00003B/133/P